Sólo Rostros
(Only faces)

Luciano Trigos

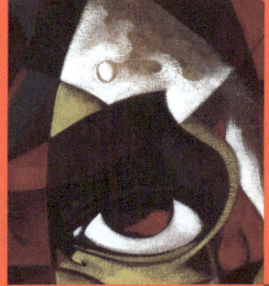
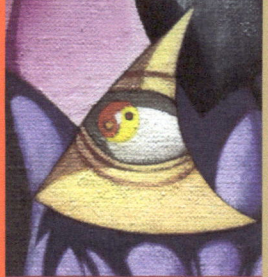
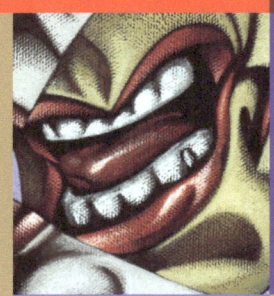
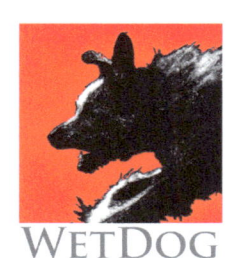

WetDog

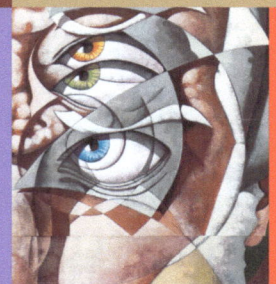

Autorretrato
Oil / Paper
1990's

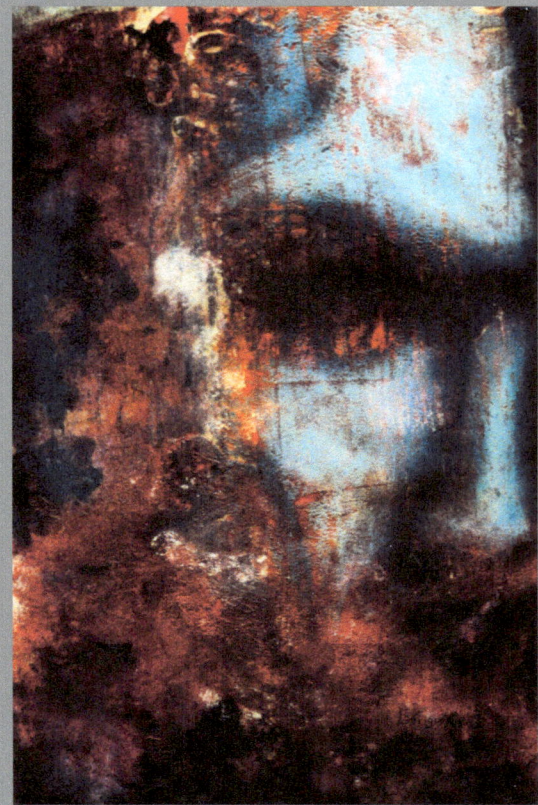

Sólo Rostros
Only faces

Luciano Trigos

Paintings by Luciano Trigos
Layout & Cover: WetDog

Pintura de Luciano Trigos
Maqueta y portada: WetDog

ISBN: 9798358609815

www.hemoficcion.com/luciano-trigos-pintura
opensea.io/LucianoTrigos
opensea.io/Wet-Dog

All Rights reserved, including de right of reproducción in whole or in part in any form.

Copyright © 2022 Luciano Trigos

GLOSSARY (*Glosario*)

Mixed technique	Técnica mixta
Enamel	Esmalte sintético
Canvas	Tela / Lienzo
Oil	Óleo
Cardboard	Cartulina
Acrylic	Acrílico
Woodcut	Xilografía
Wood panel	Panel de madera
Canvas board	Cartón con tela
Ranting	Despotricando
Hemofiction	Hemoficción

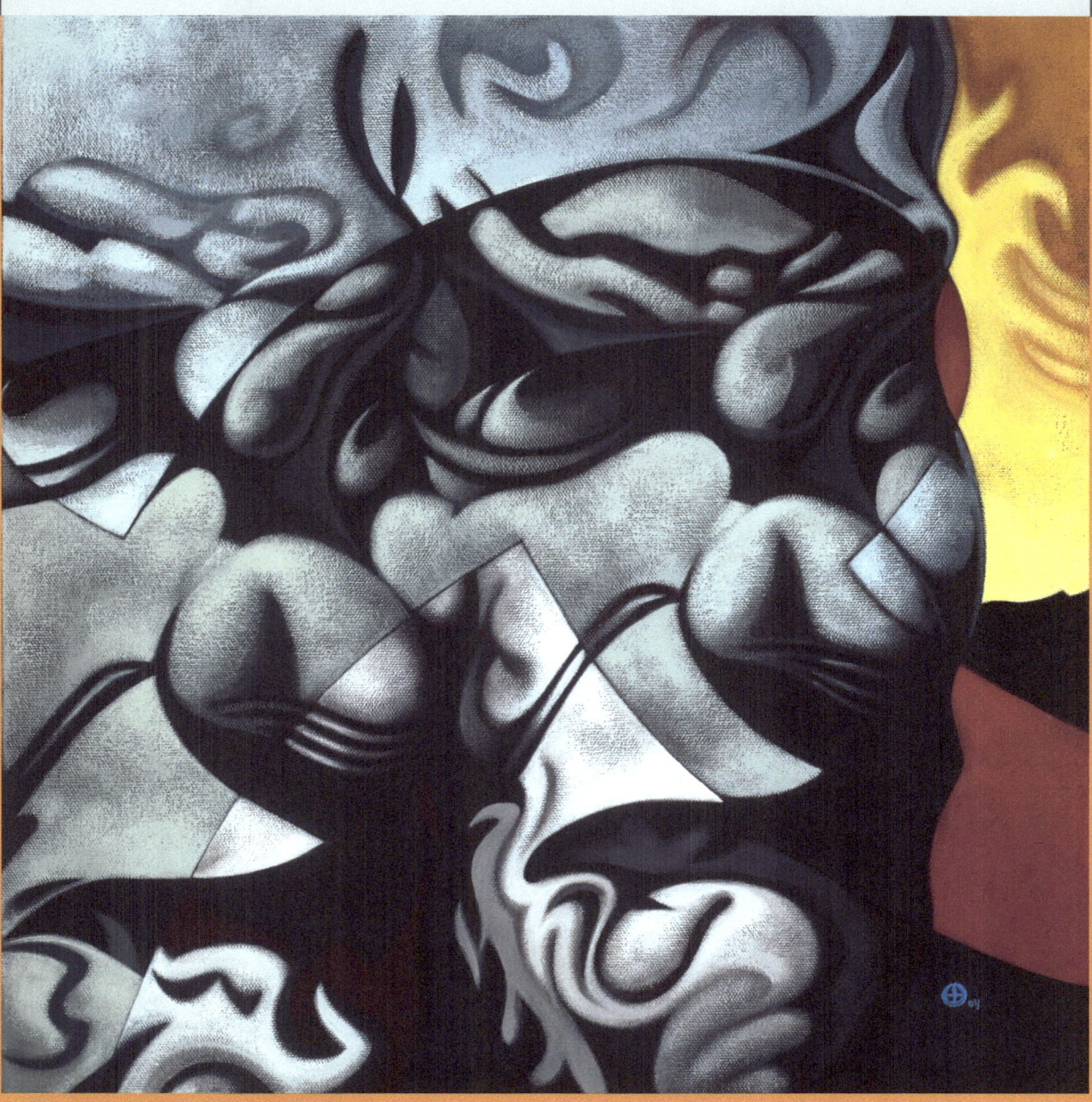

Hemofictions 3
Enamel / Canvas
16" X 16"
2004

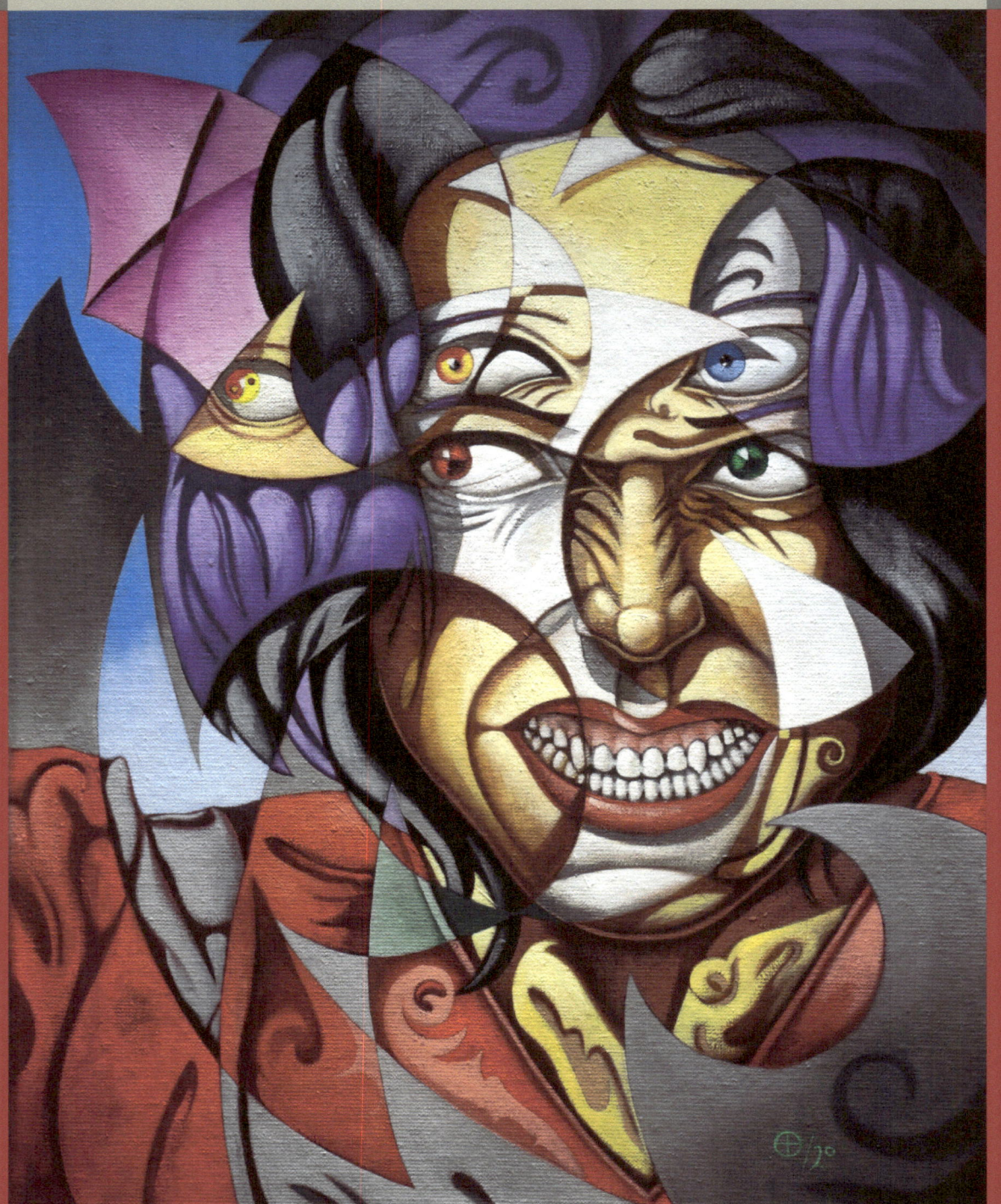

Jaca
oil / Canvas
20" x 16"
2020

Submerged-Head
Enamel / Canvas
36" x 24"
2005

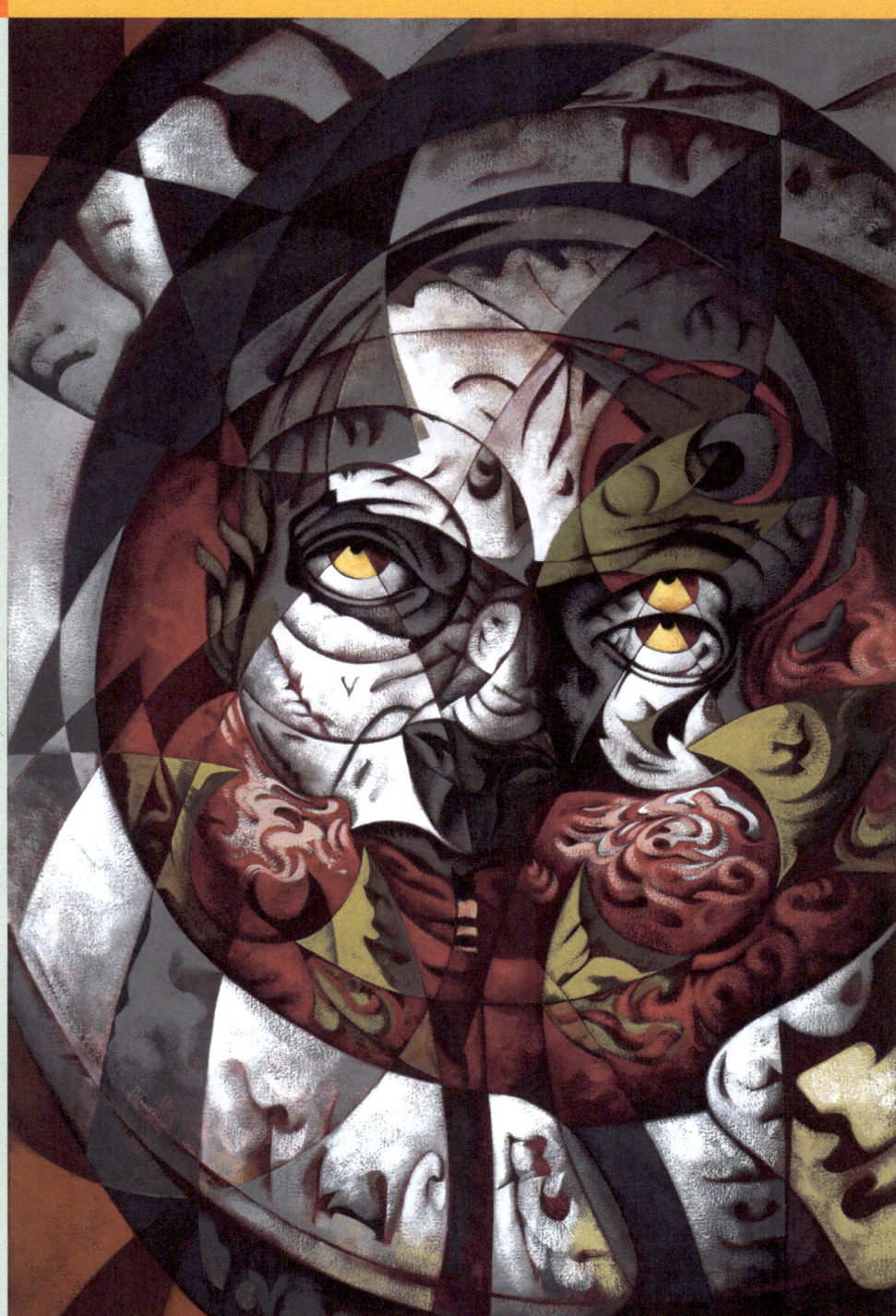

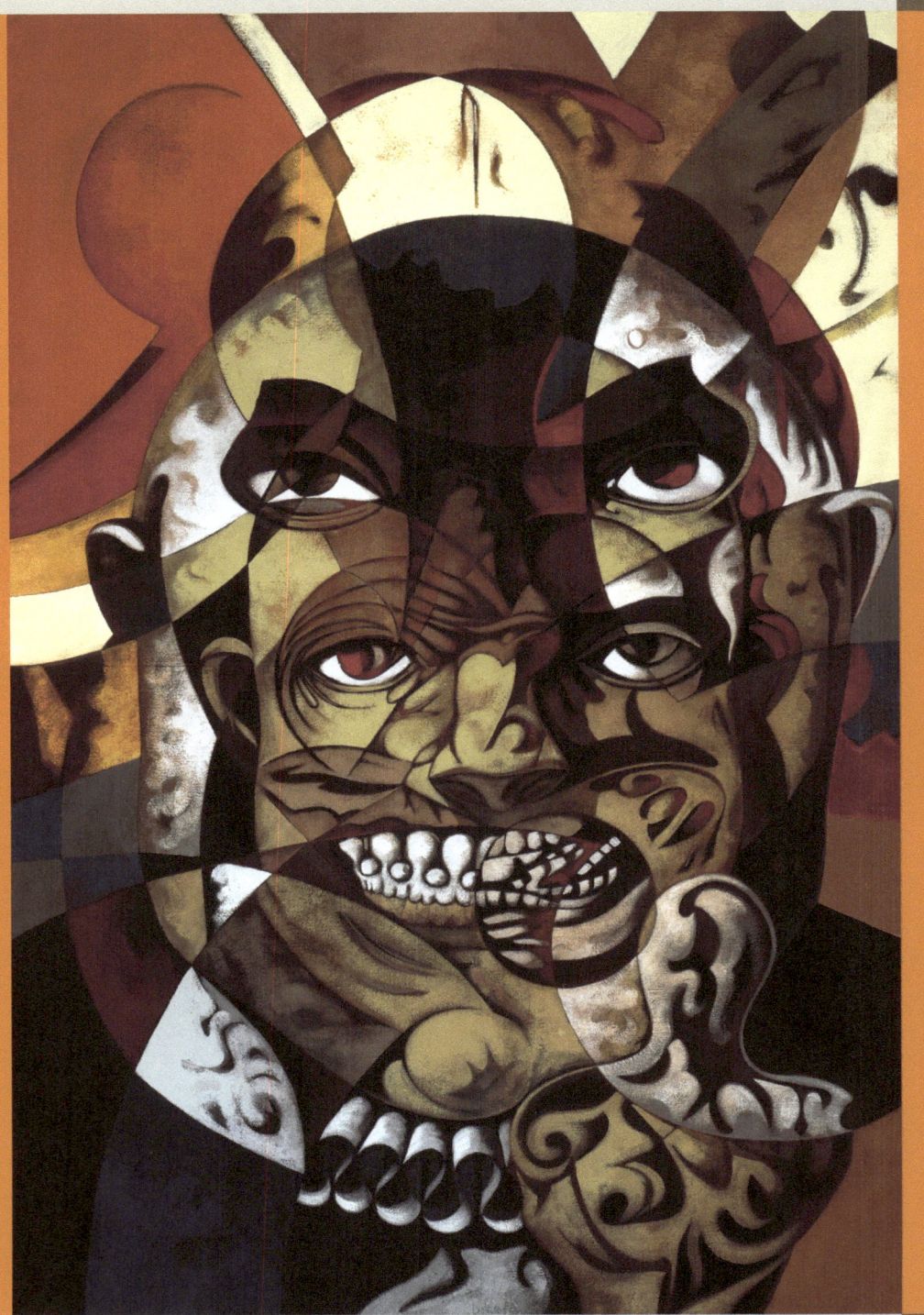

Double Head
Enamel / Canvas
36" x 24"
2005

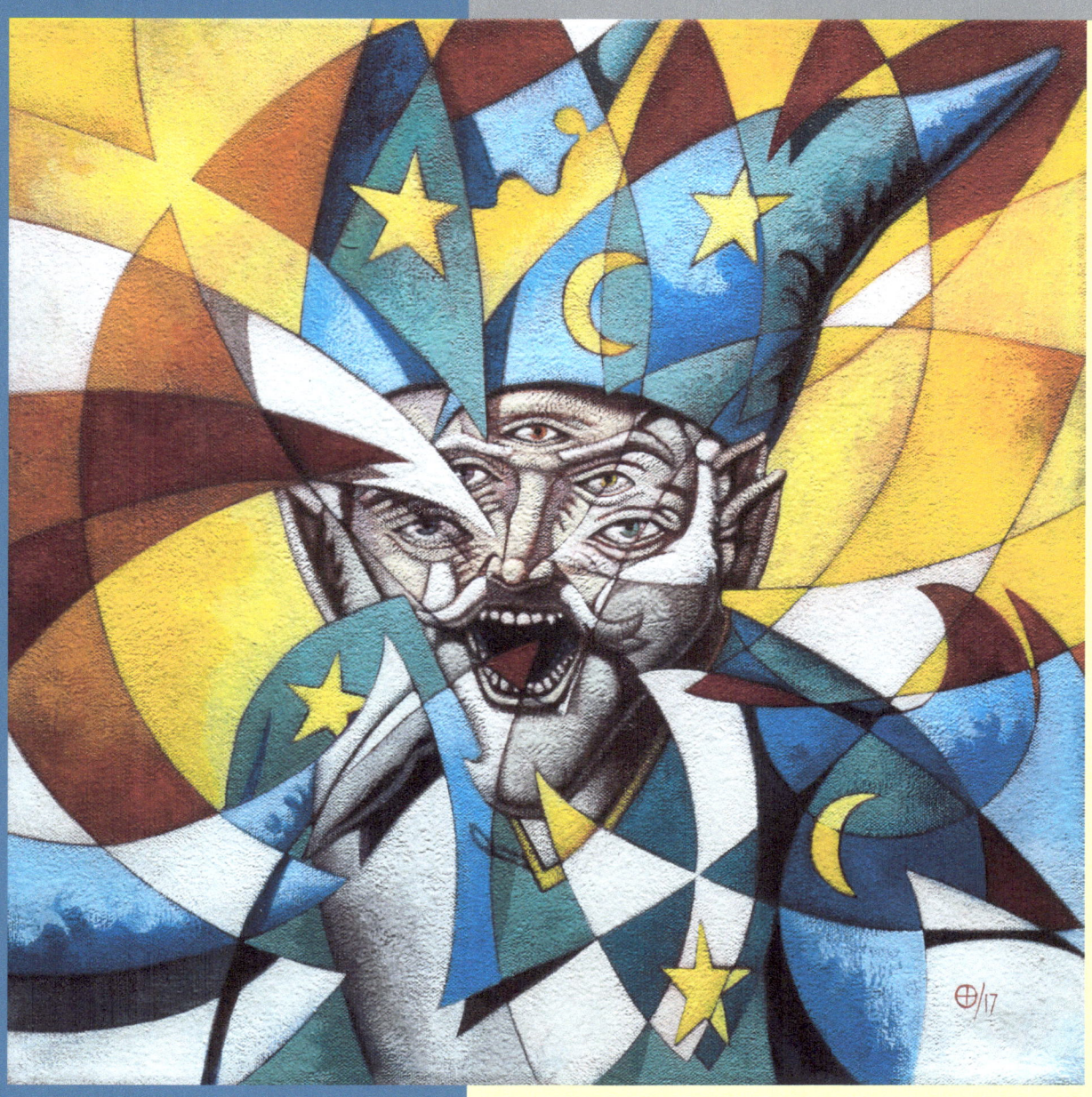

Merlín
Enamel / Canvas
40 cm x 40 cm
2017

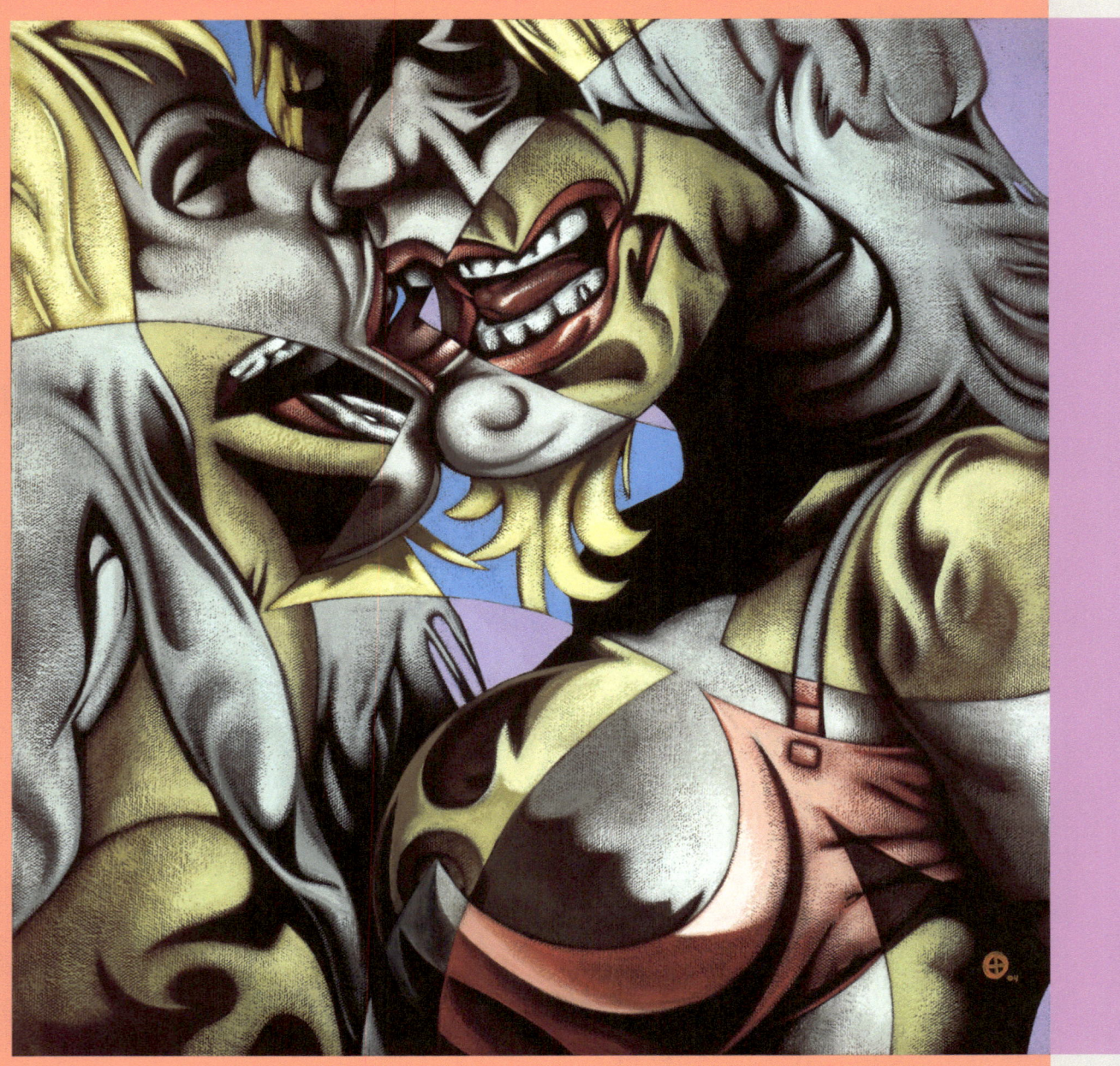

Hemofictions 1
Enamel / Canvas
16" X 16"
2004

Dama plural
Oil / Canvas
36" x 24"
2021

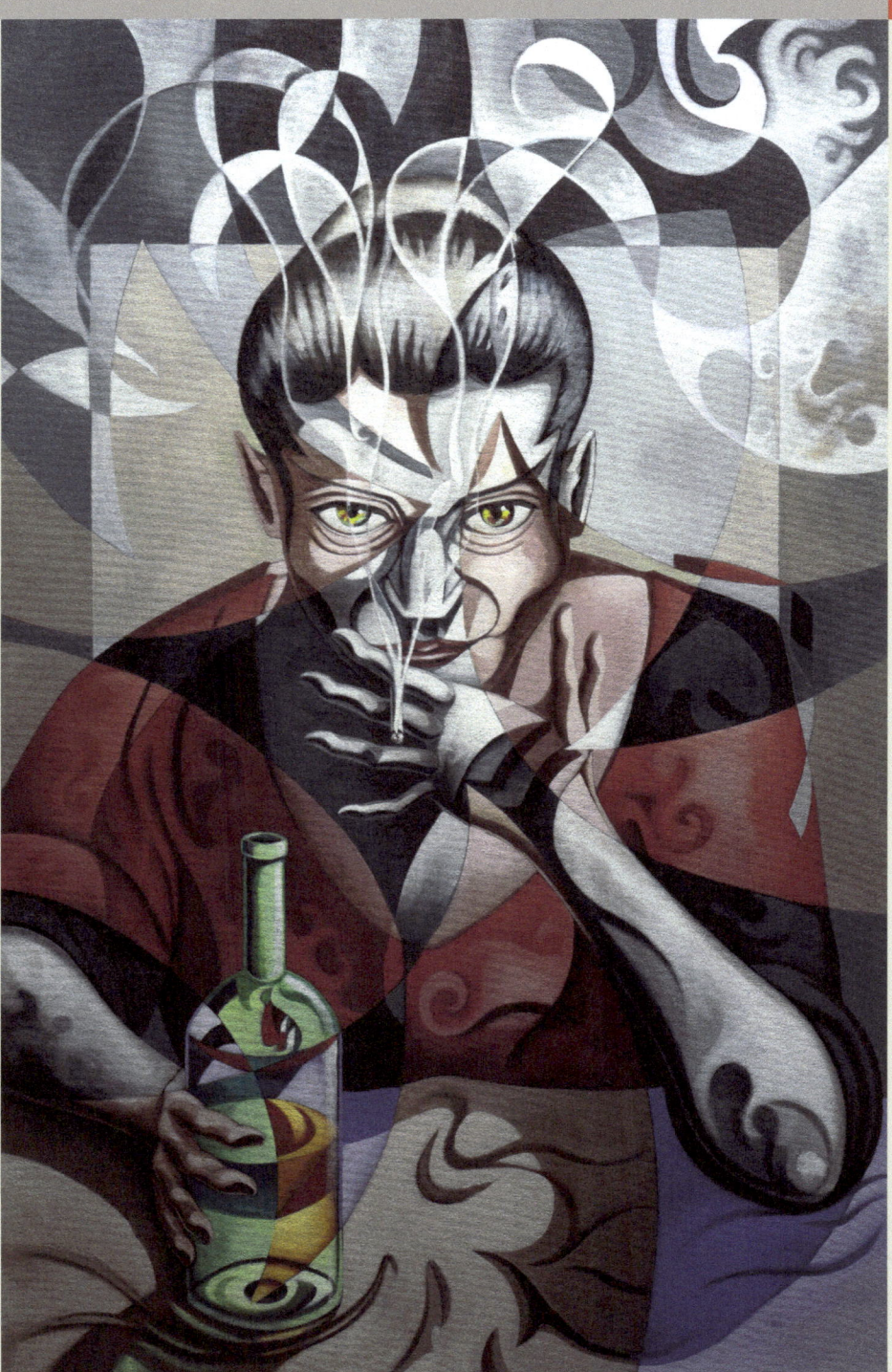

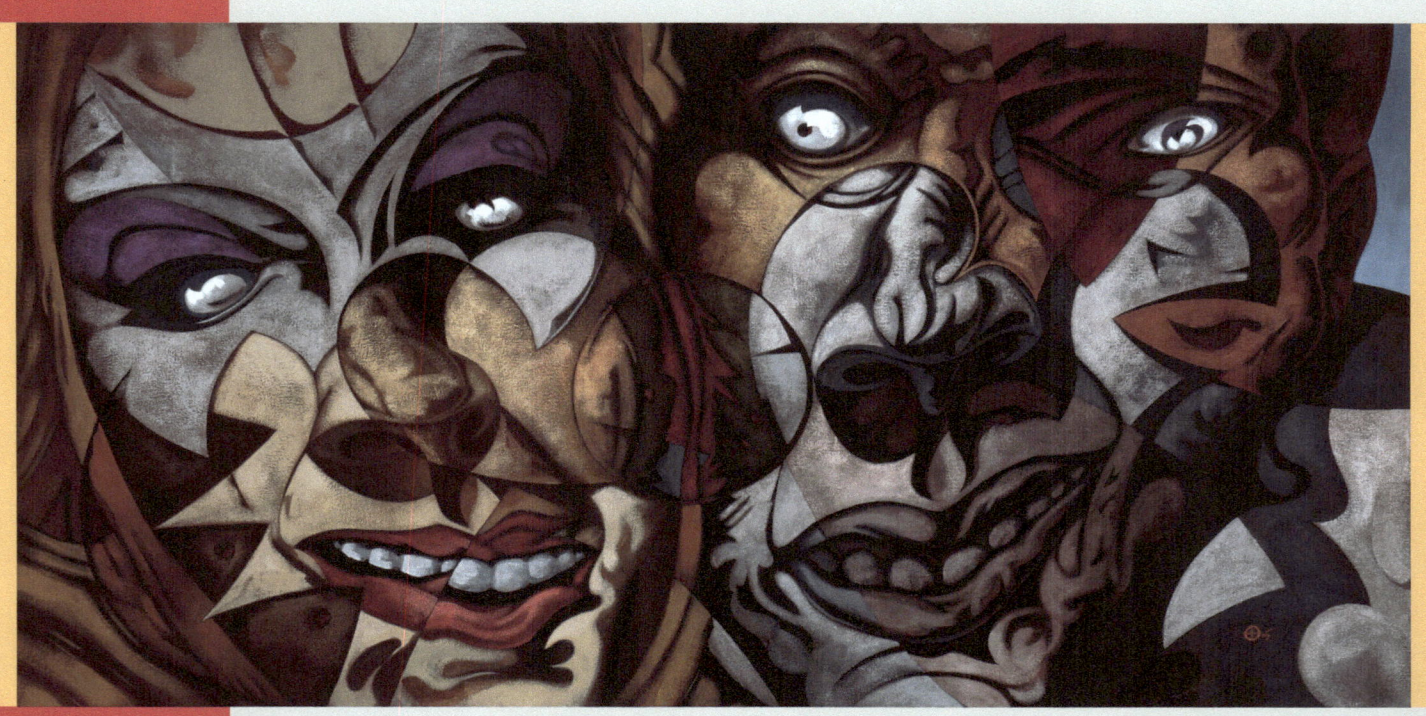

Hemofictions 4
Enamelo / Canvas
24" X 48"
2005

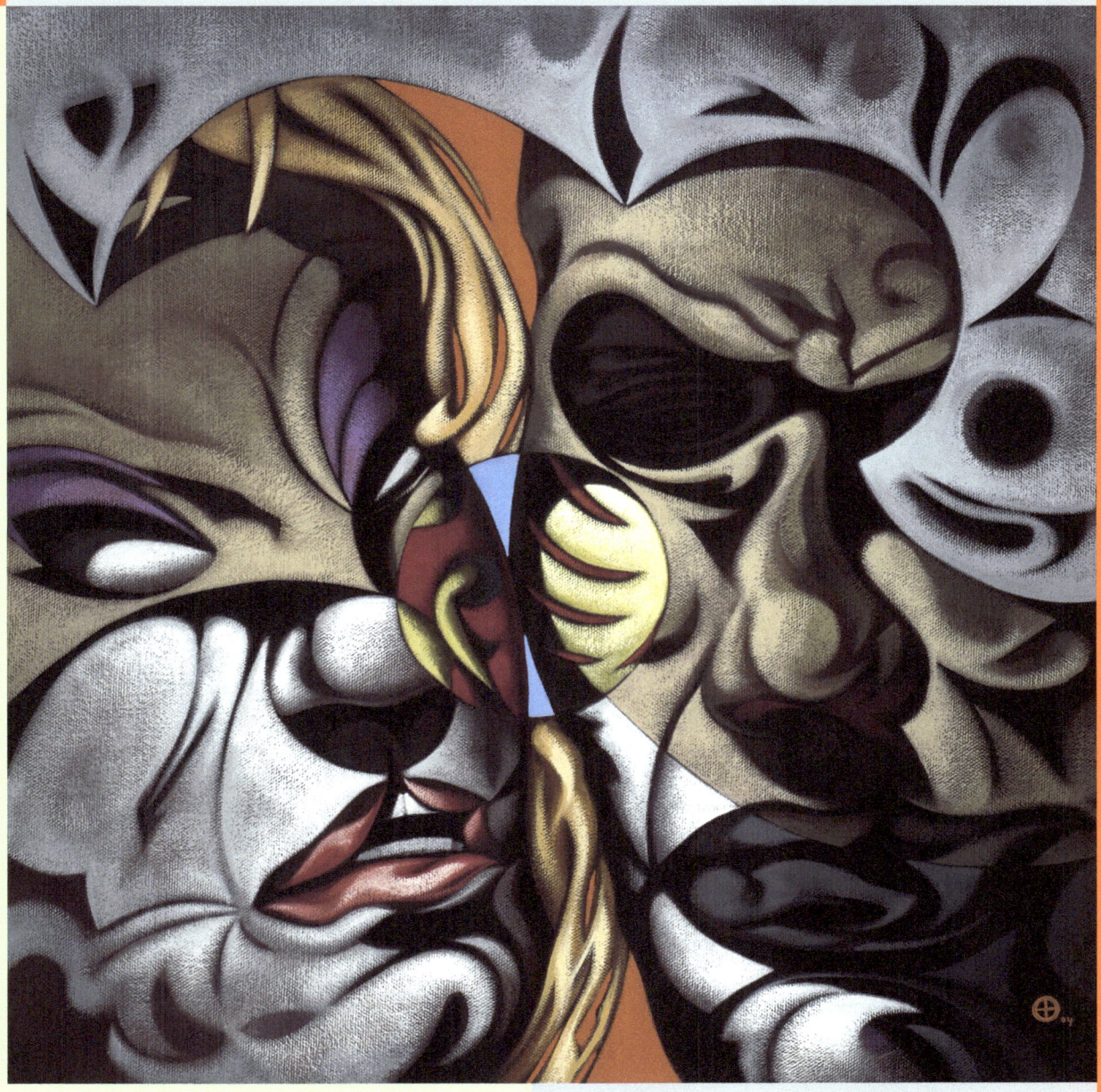

Hemofictions 2
Enamel / Canvas
16" X 16"
2004

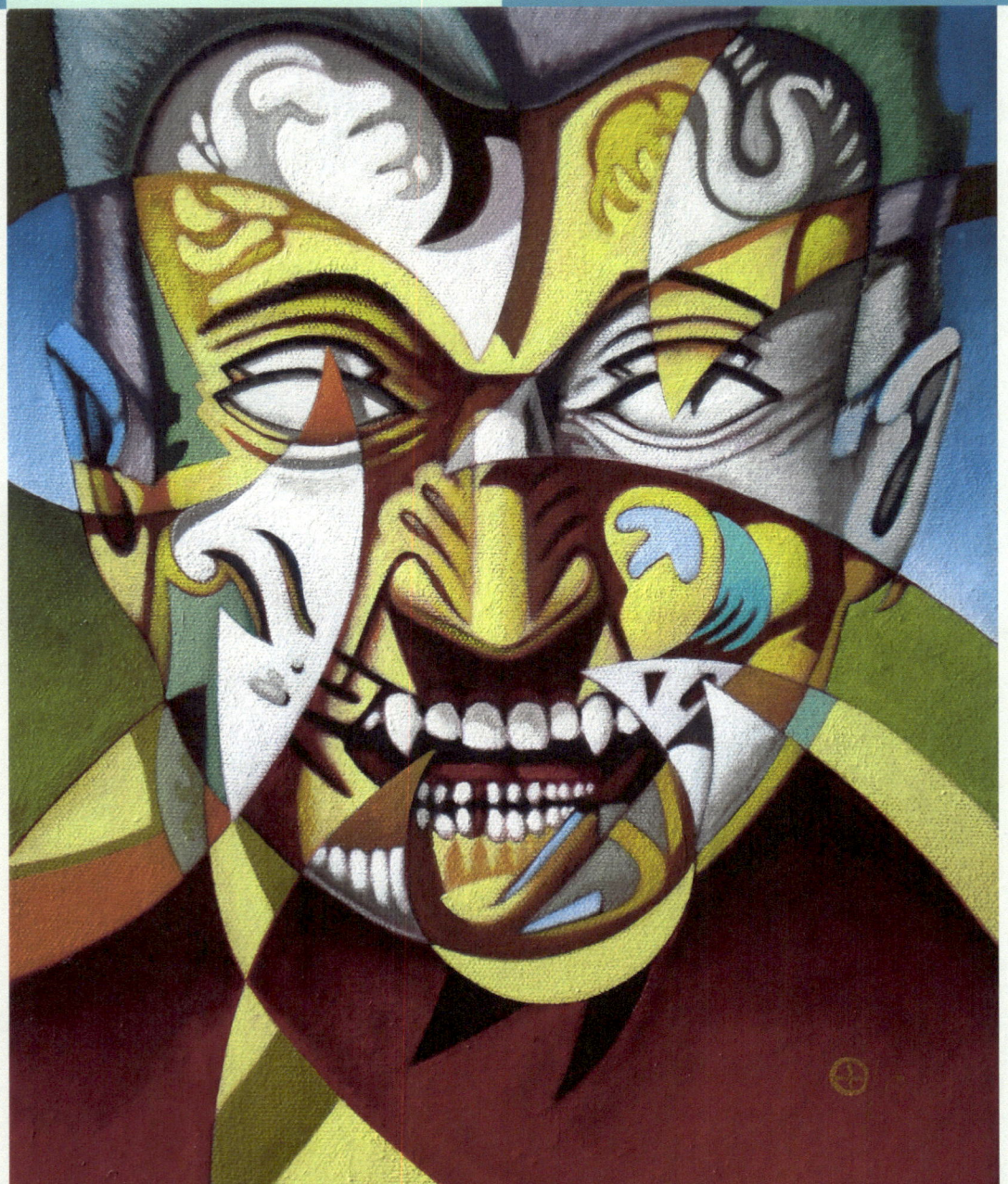

Rostro dentado I
Oil / Canvas
30 cm x 25 cm
2017

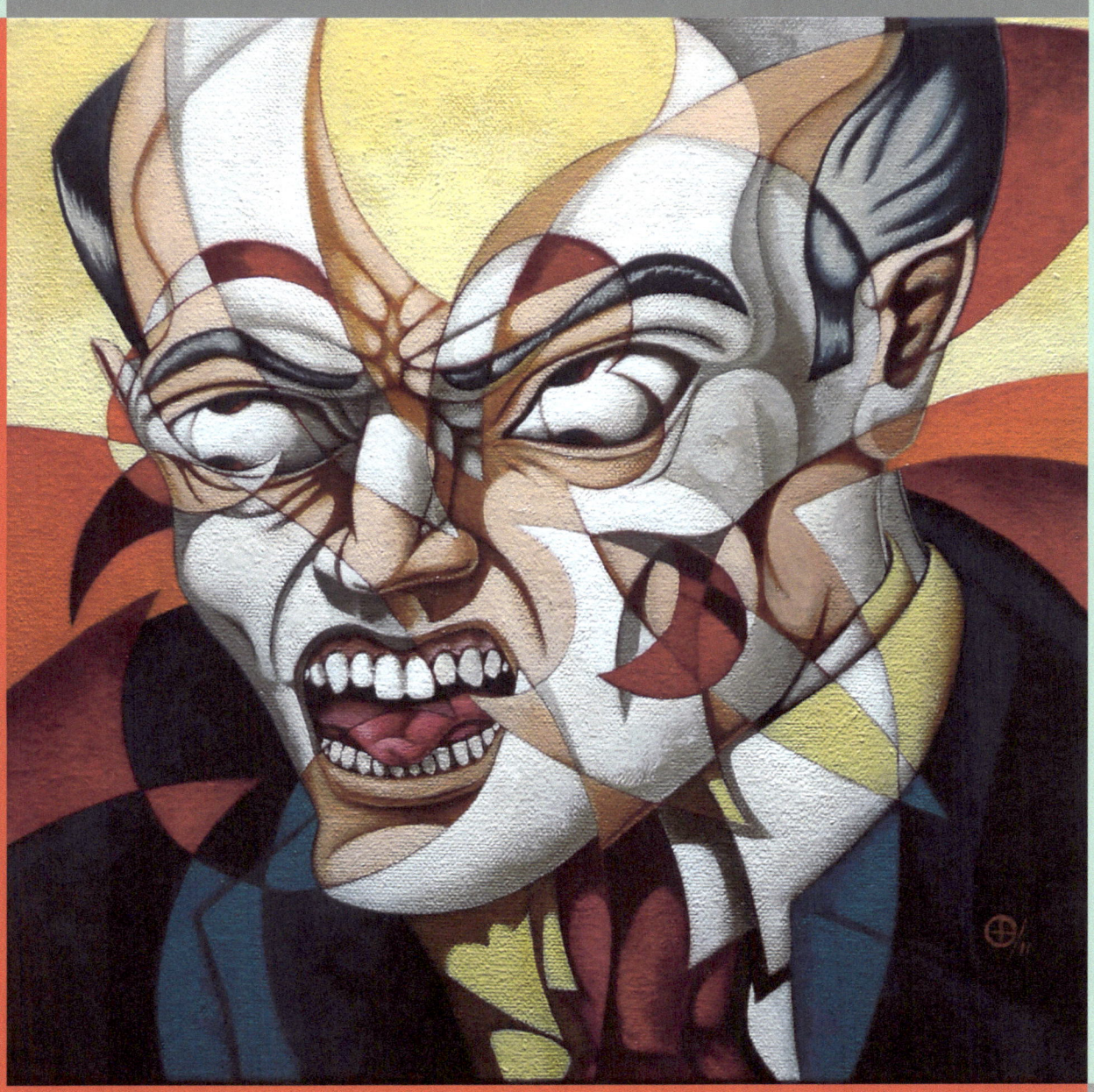

Ranting Hemofiction
Oil / Canvas
12" x 12"
2011

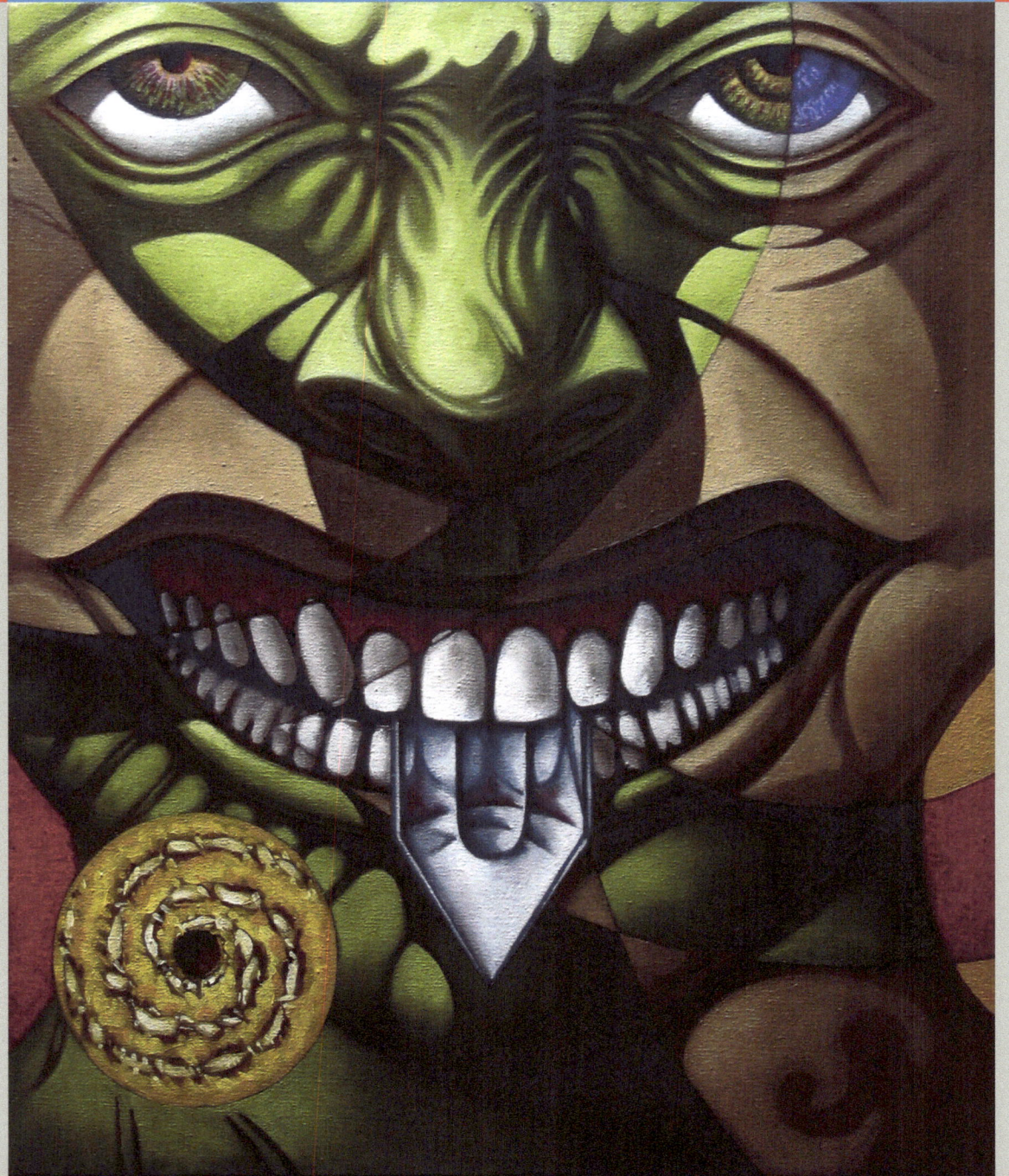

Sword tongue
Oil / Canvas
25 cm x 20 cm
2008

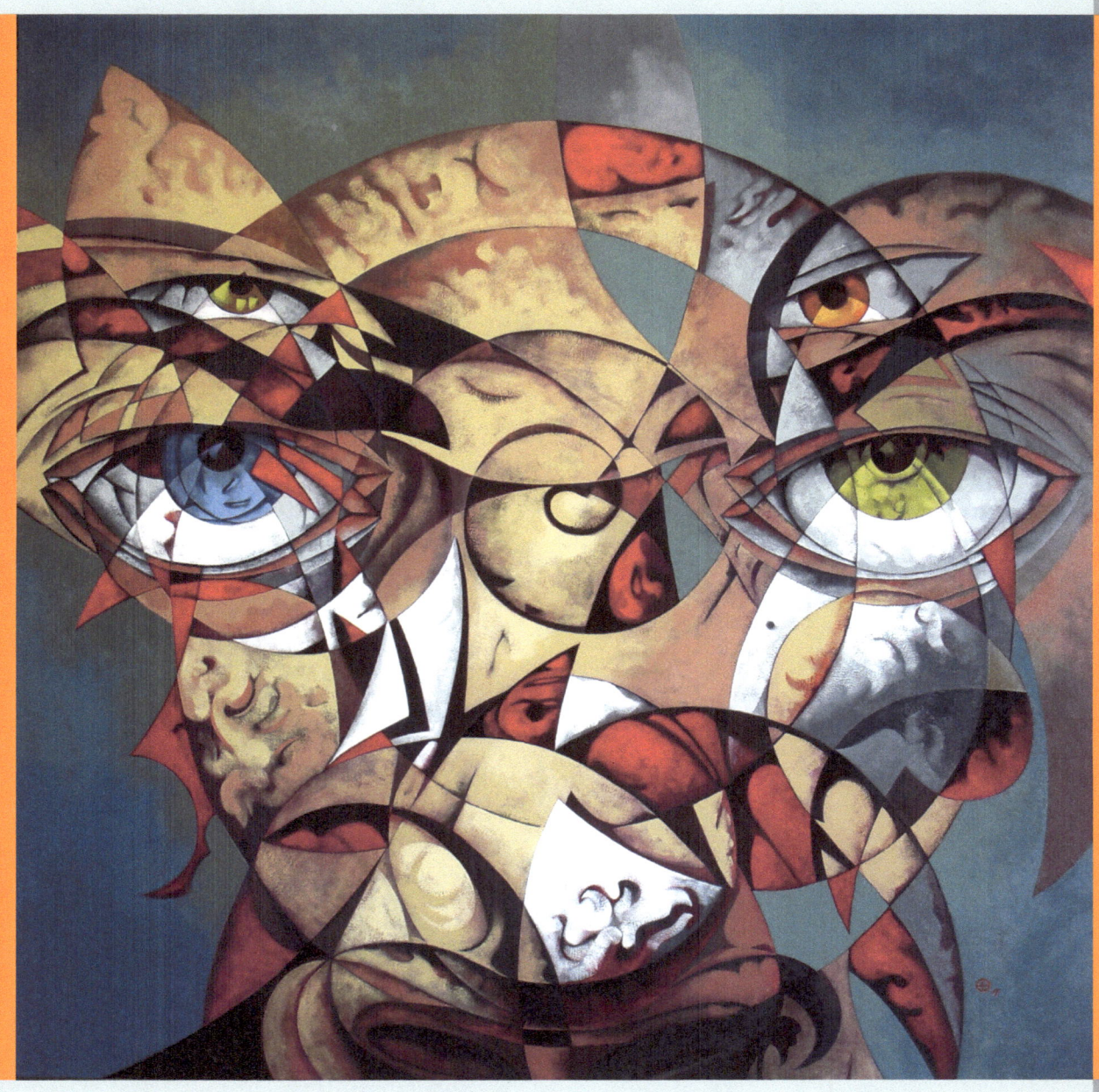

Hemofictions 13
Enamel / Canvas
48" x 48"
2007

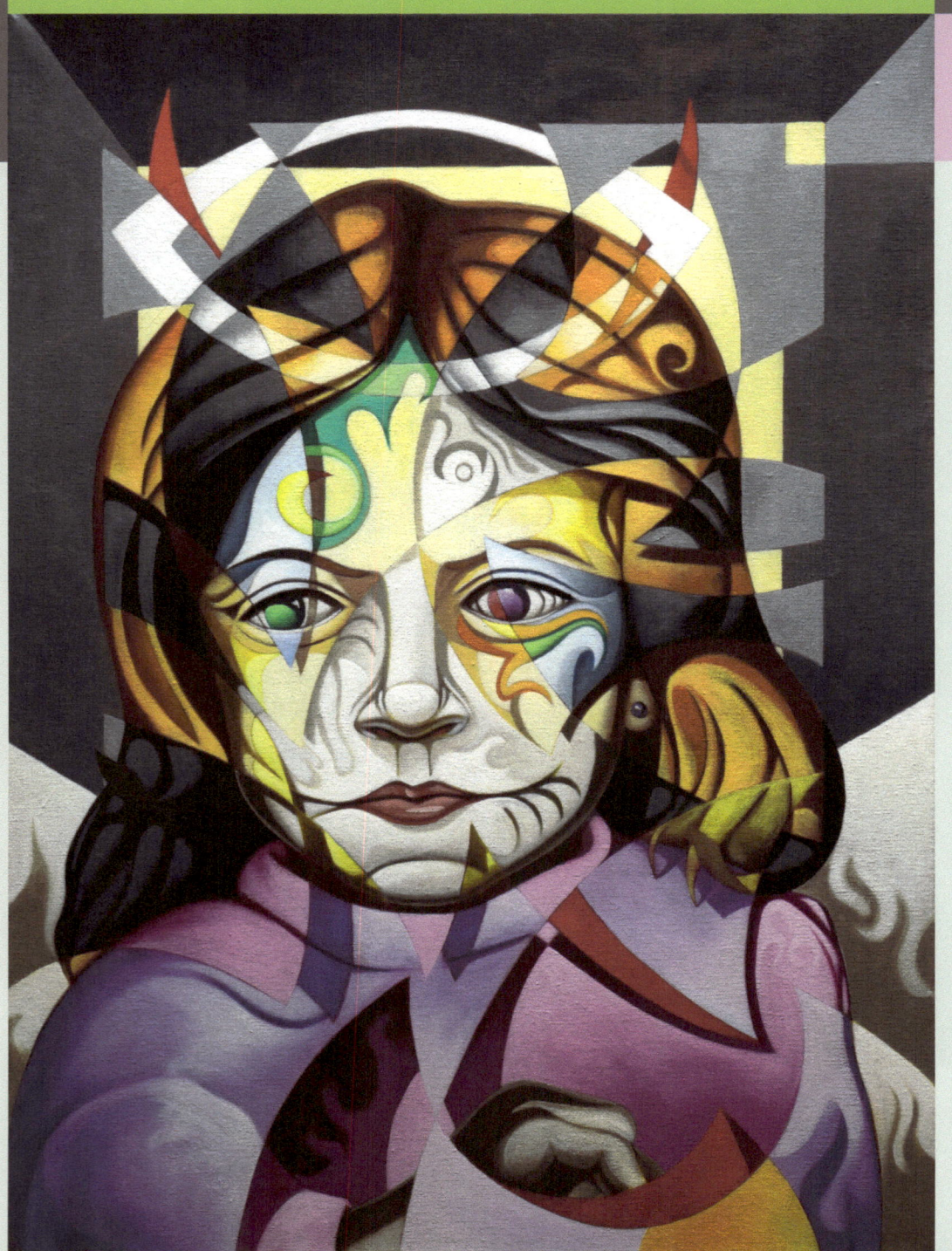

Ánima tangible
Oil / Canvas
60 cm x 45 cm
2020

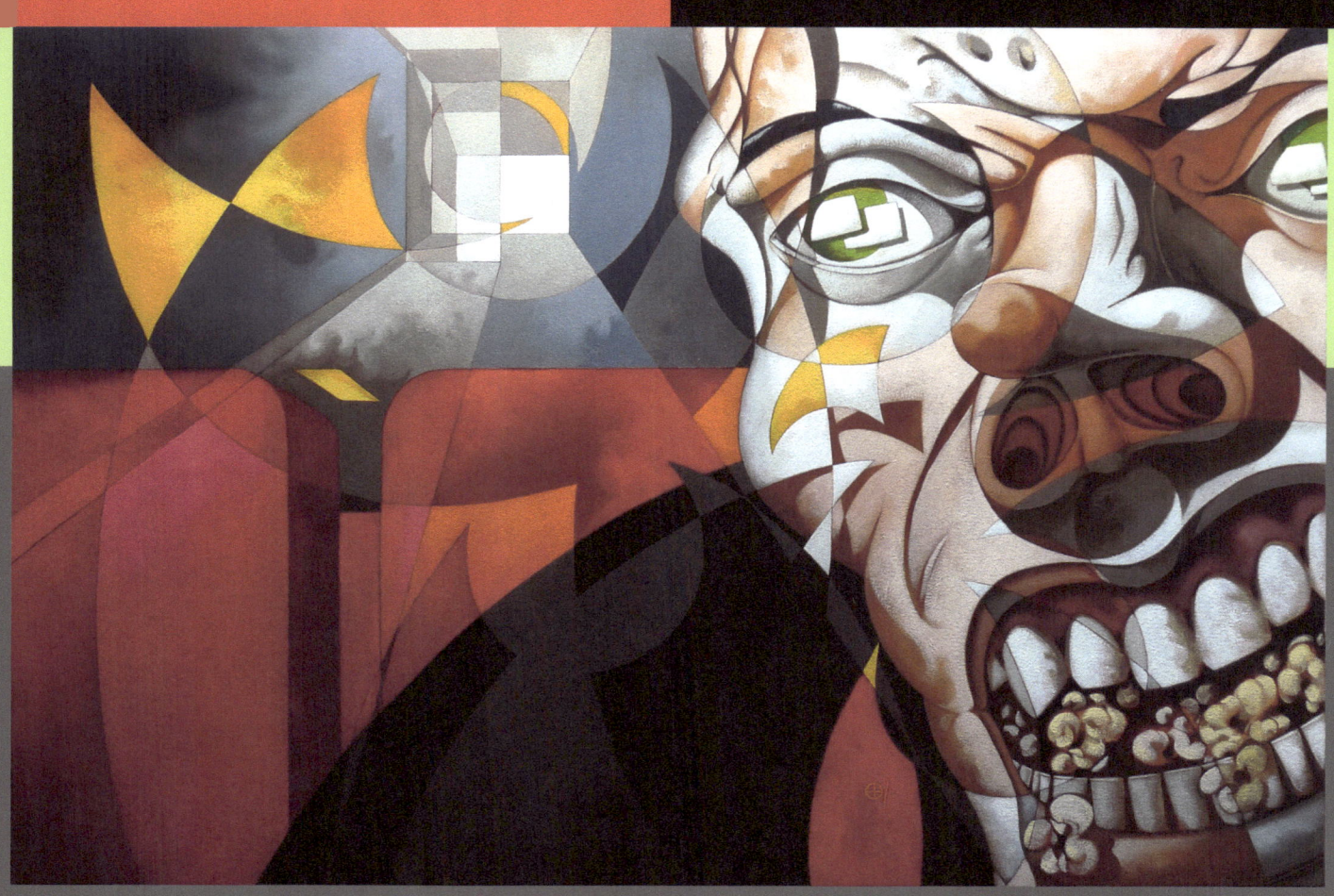

Hemofiction at sight
Oil / Canvas
24" x 36"
2011

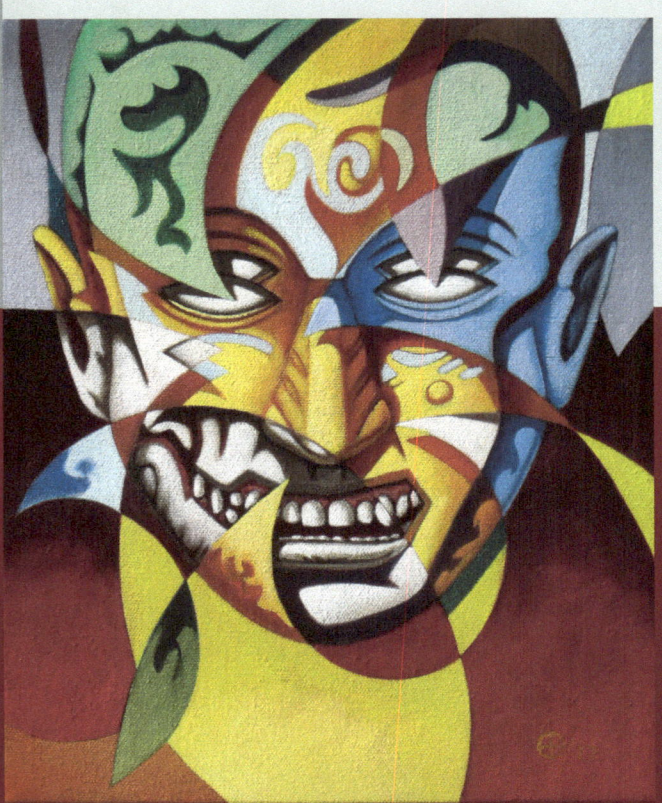

Rostro dentado II
Oil / Canvas
30 cm X 25 cm
2017

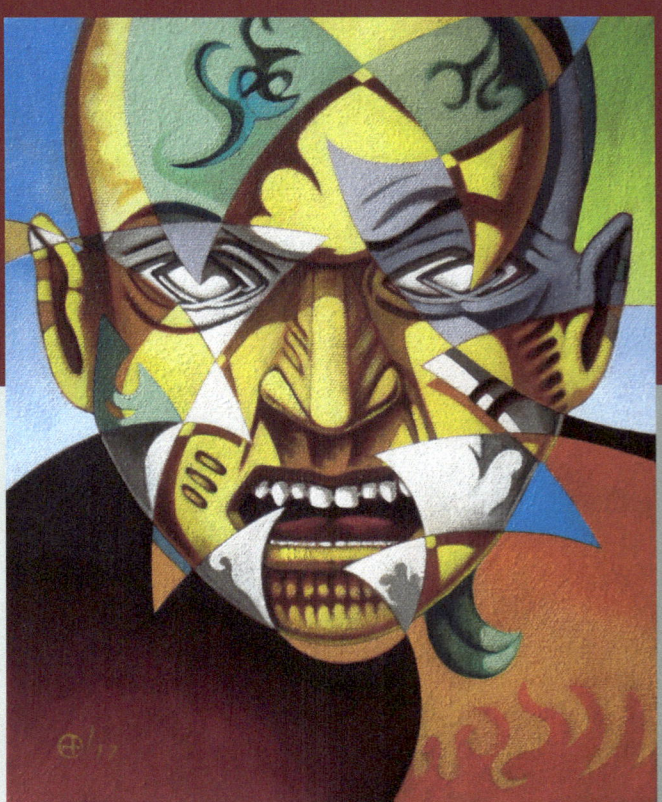

Rostro dentado III
Oil / Canvas
30 cm X 25 cm
2017

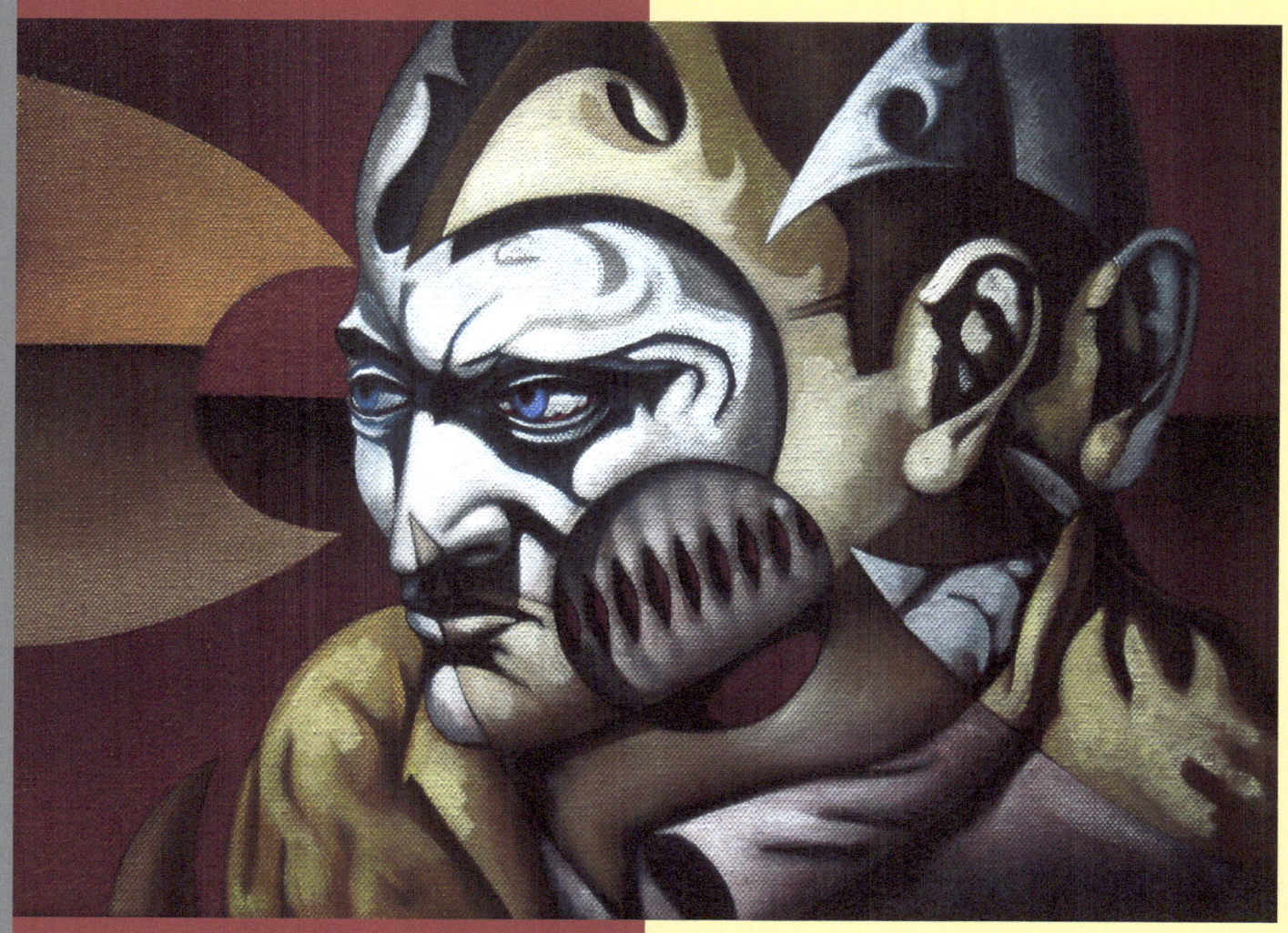

Resonancia humana
Oil / Canvas
2008

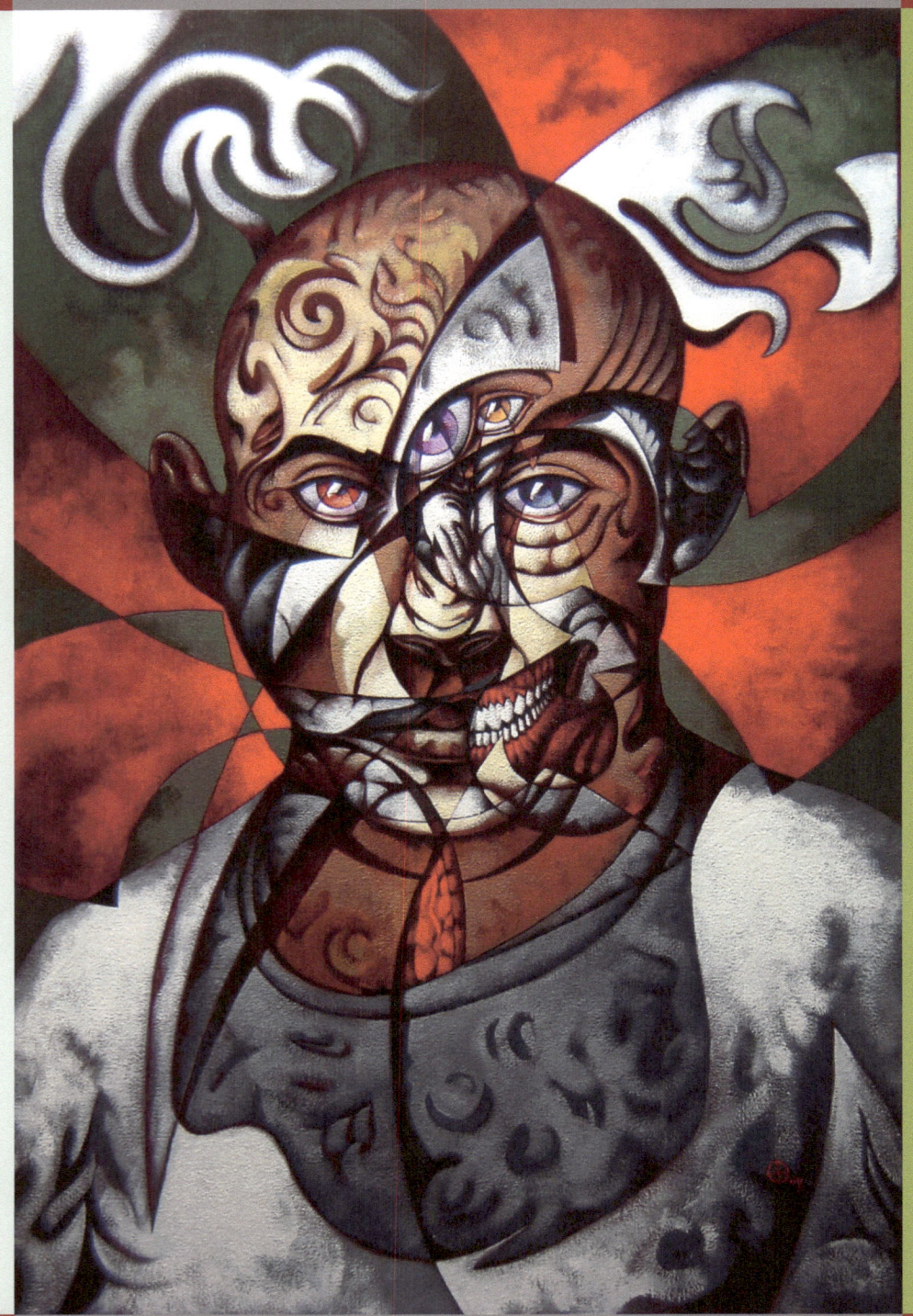

Self portrait
Enamel / Canvas
36" x 24"
2009

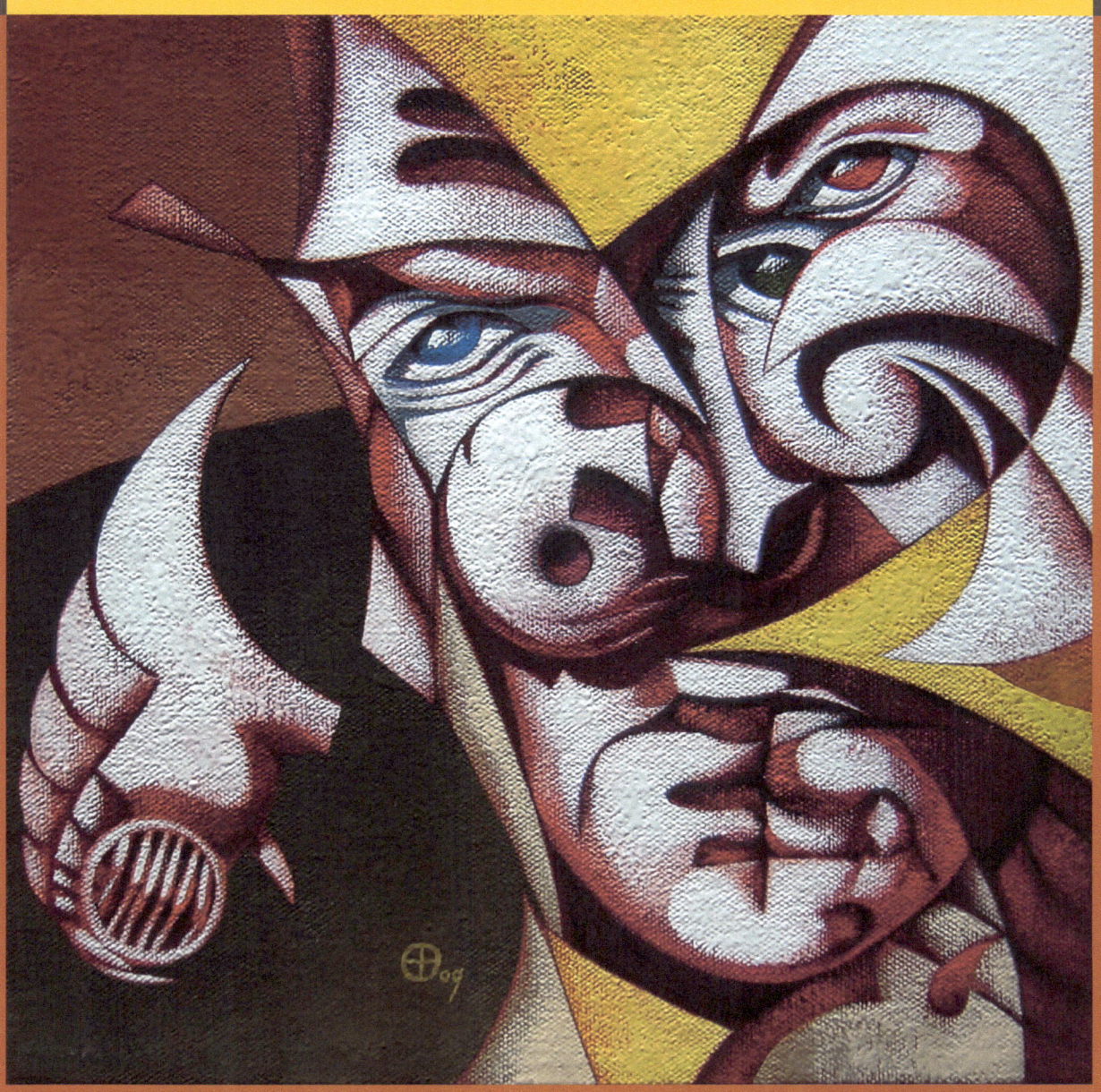

Hemofictions 16
Enamel / Canvas
10" x 10"
2009

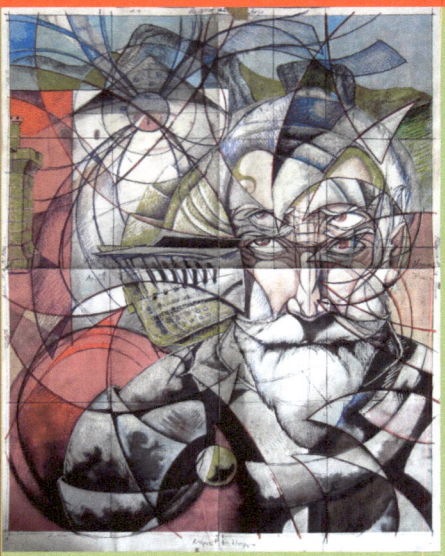

SKETCH
DRAWING / PAPER
22" X 17"
2012

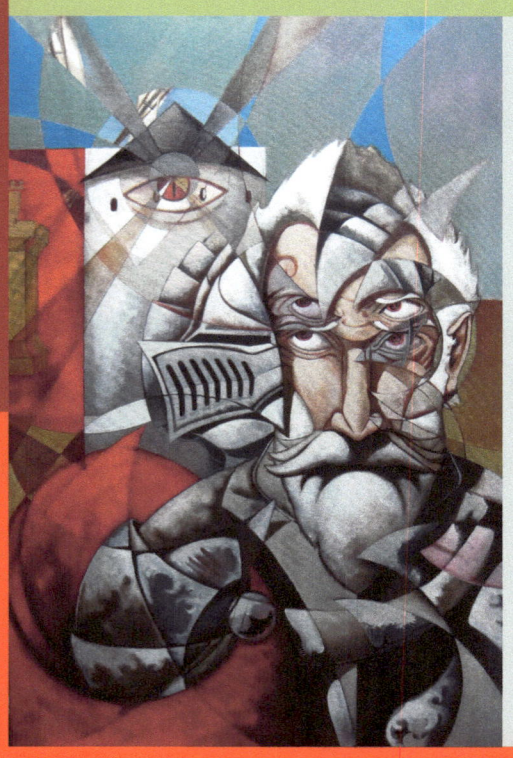

SKETCH
OIL / CANVAS
36" X 24"
2012

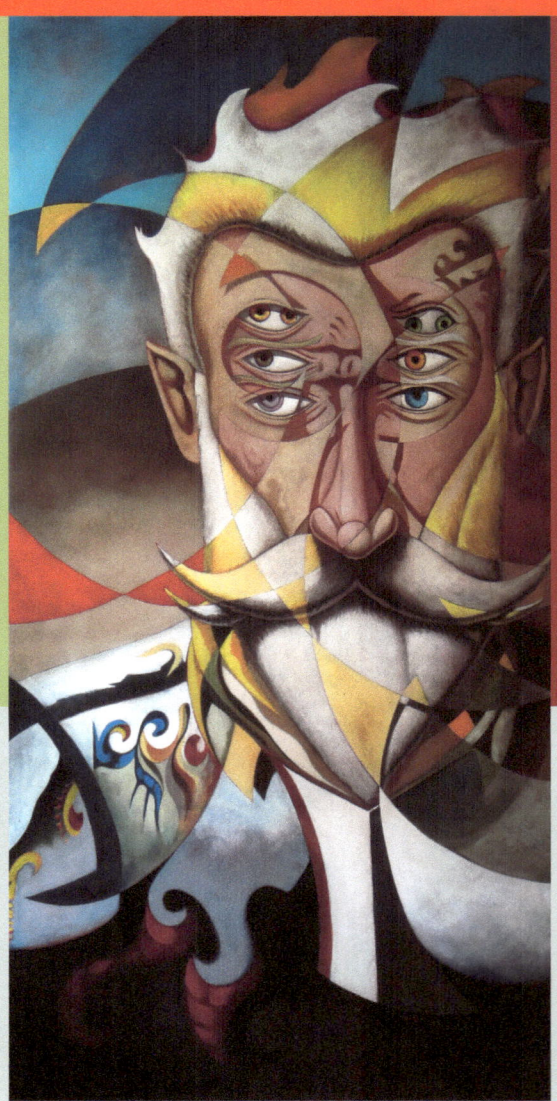

QUIJOTE
OIL / CANVAS
190 CM X 95 CM
2015

Triptych Mural: Cervantinismos (Central panel, El Gigante)
Enamel / Wood panels
23 Square meters
2012

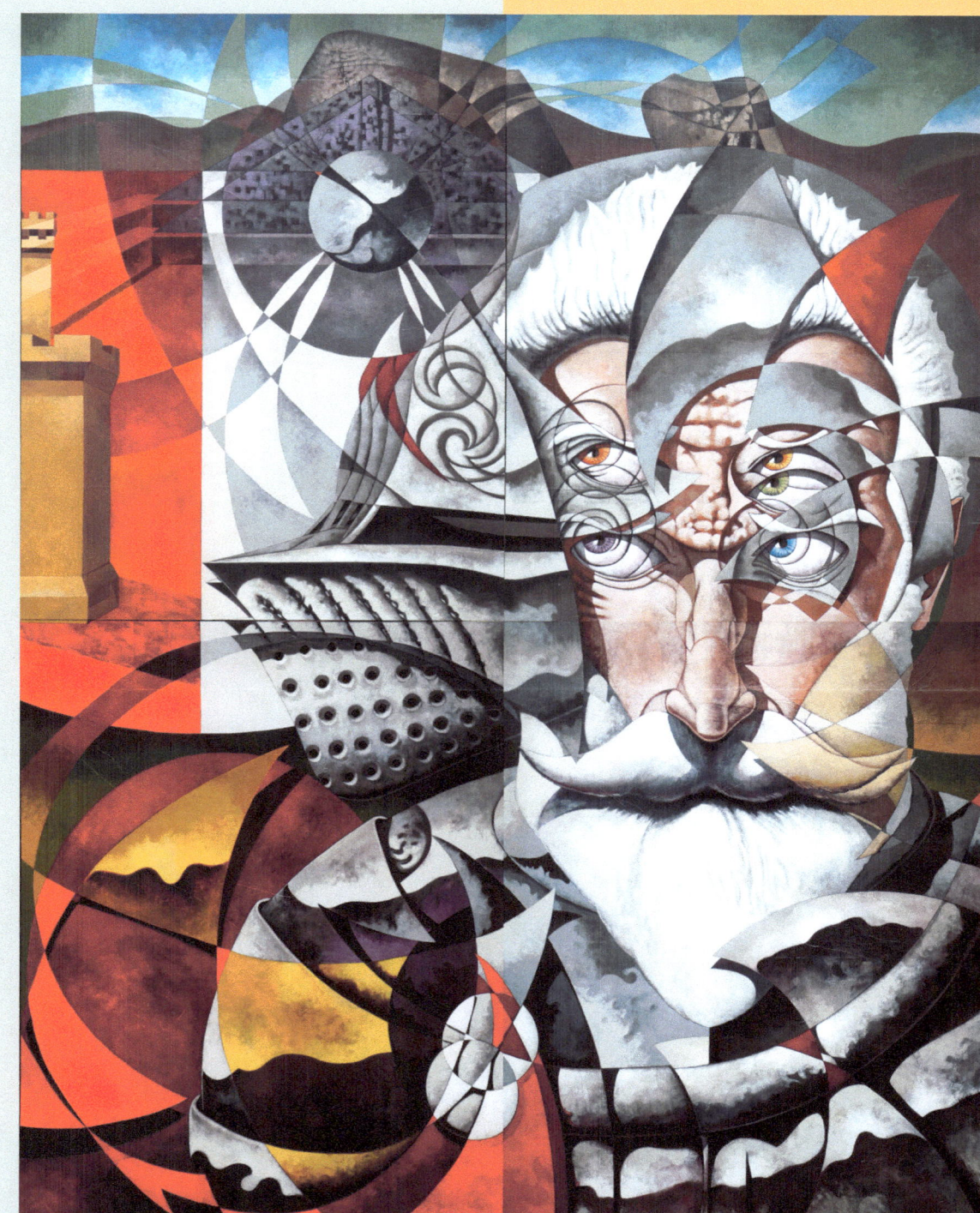

Museo Iconográfico del Quijote, Guanajuato Gto. Mex

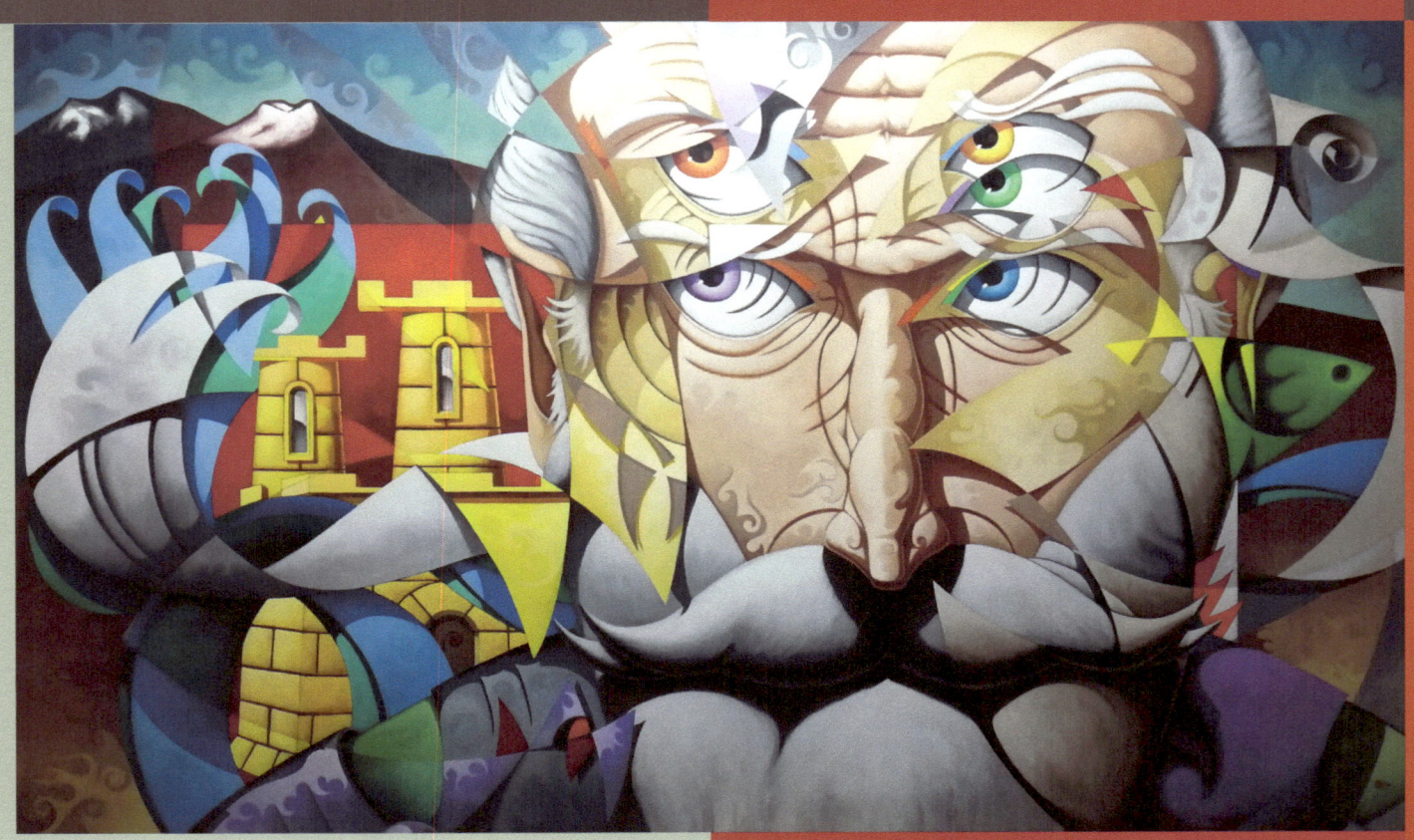

Caballero ideal
Oil / Canvas
120 cm x 200 cm
2021

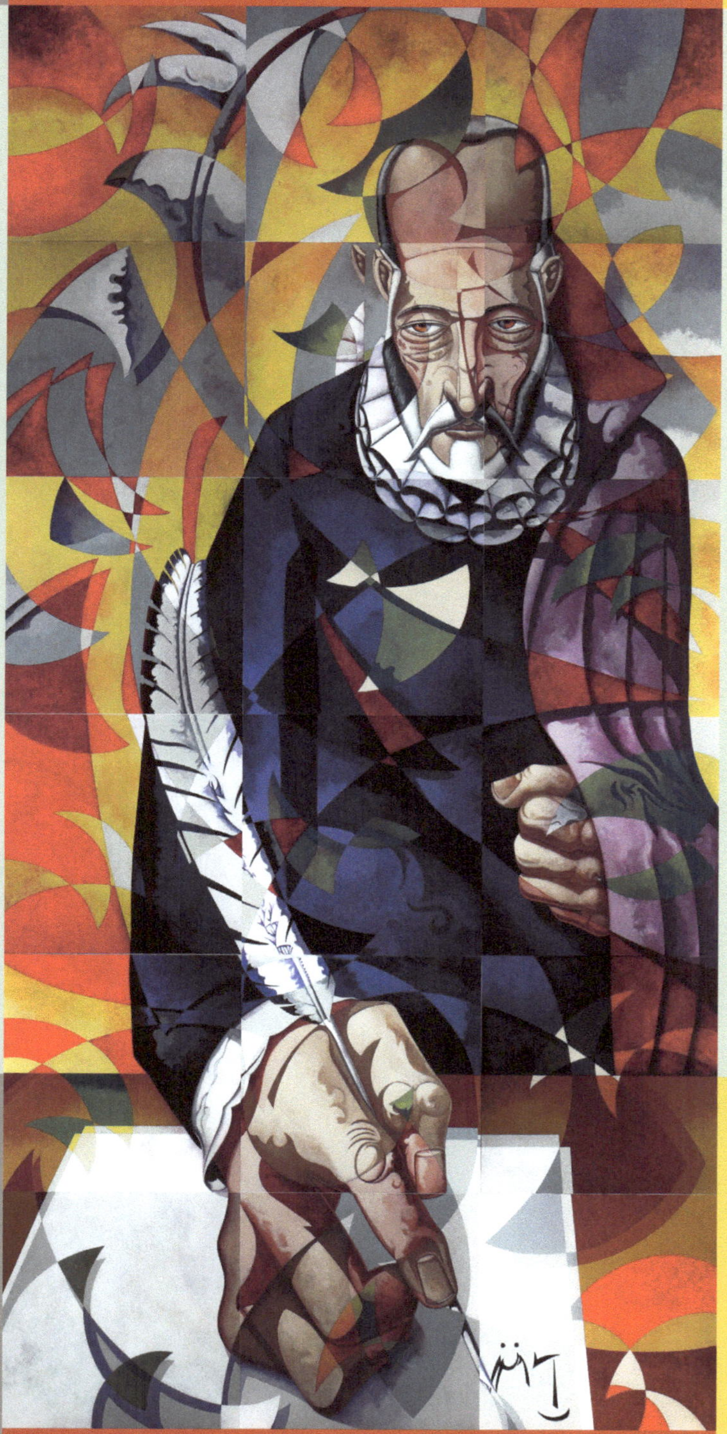

(Centro de Estudios Cervantinos, Guanajuato México)

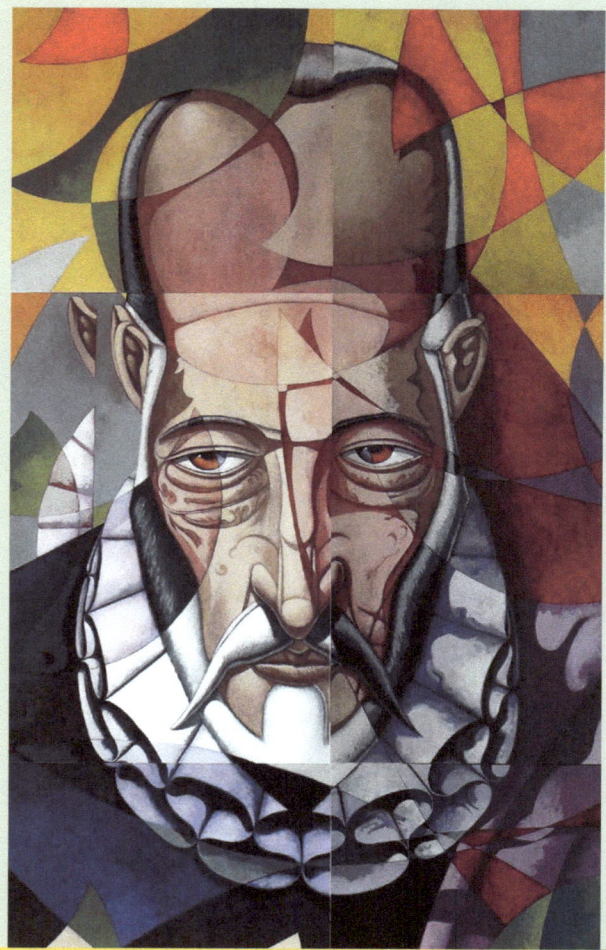

Cervantes grande plasmado en la pared
Enamel / Wood panels
600 cm x 300 cm
2015

25

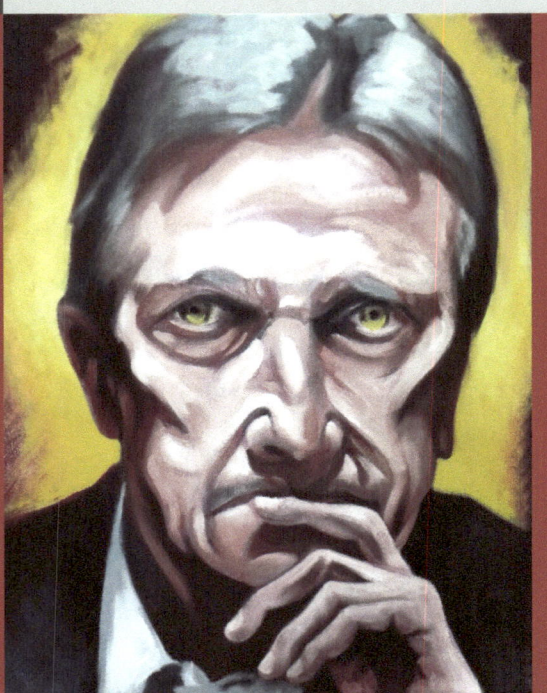

Patrick Johansson
Oil / Canvas board
40.6 cm x 30.5 cm
2022

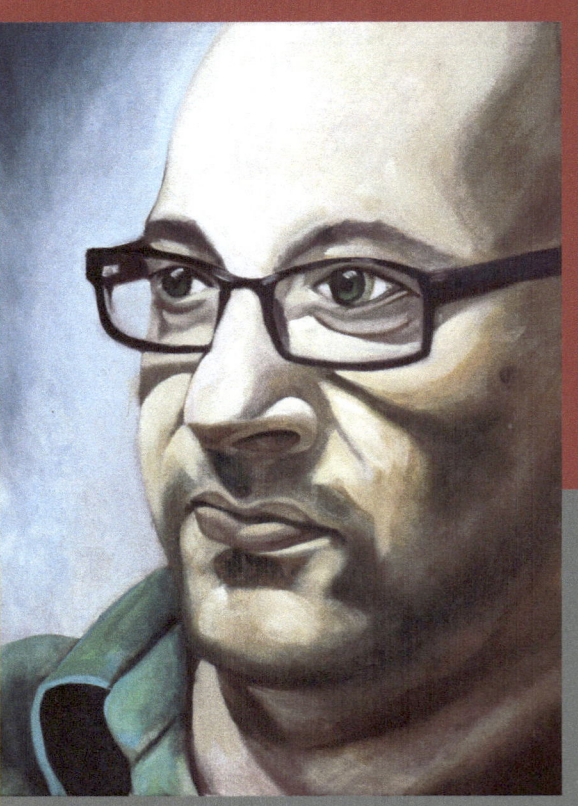

Juan Trigos R
Oil / Canvas board
40.6 cm x 30.5 cm
2022

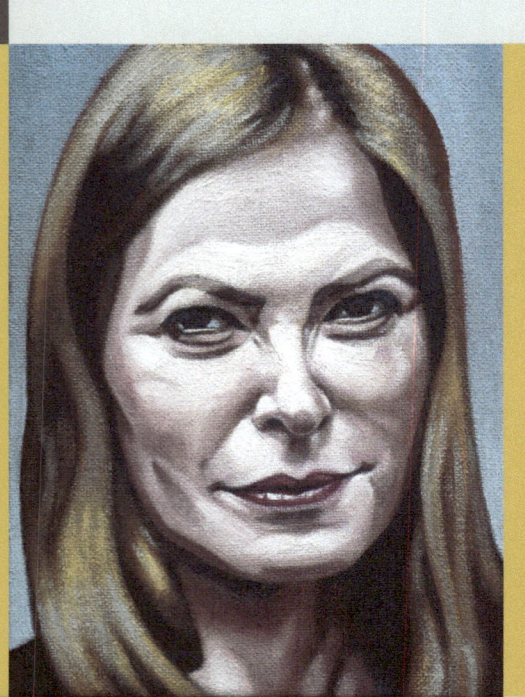

Ángela Piedad
Oil / Canvas board
20.3 cm x 15.2 cm
2022

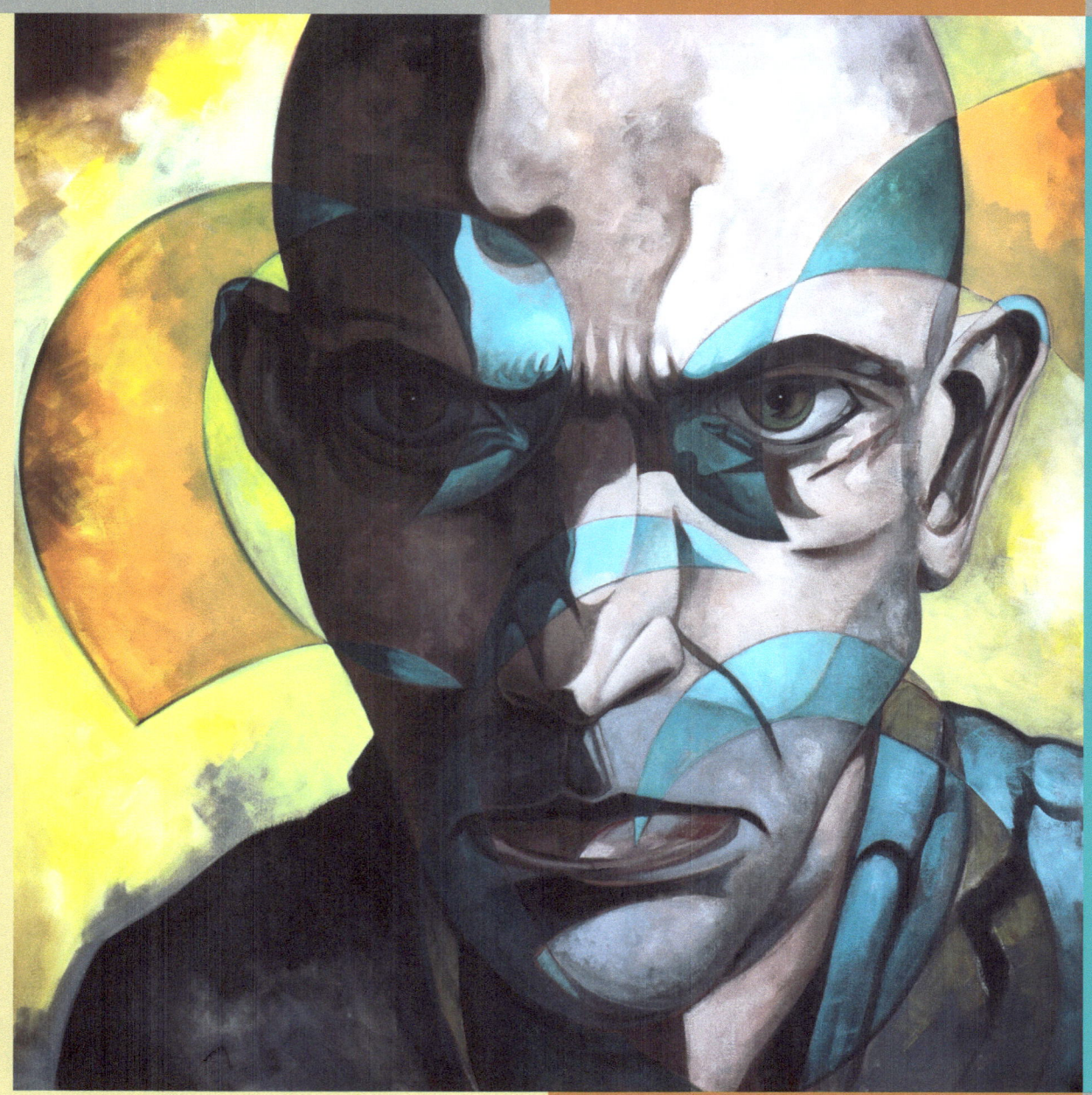

Autoretrato
Oil / Canvas
100 cm x 100 cm
2021

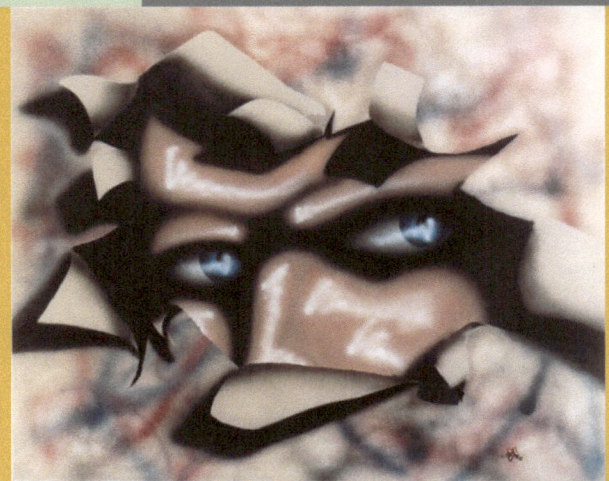

Graffiti
Acrylic / Cardboard
76 cm x 102 cm
1990

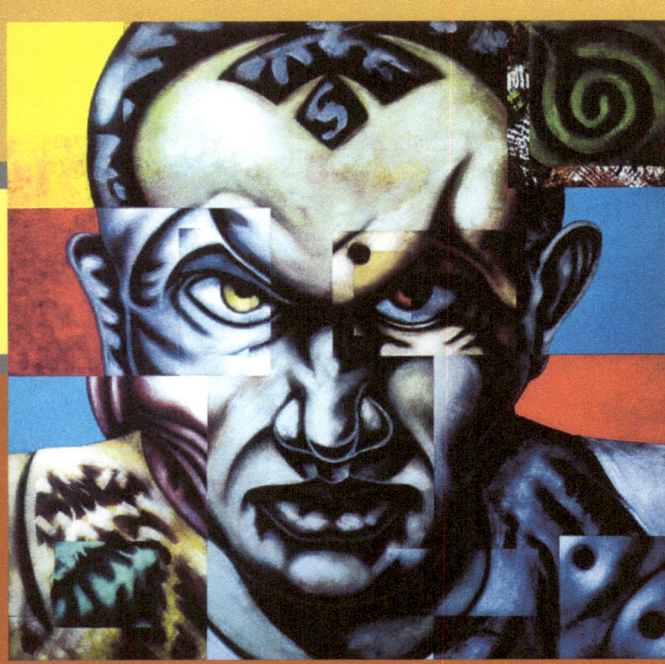

Miramiento II
Enamel / Wood panel
150 cm x 150 cm
1990's

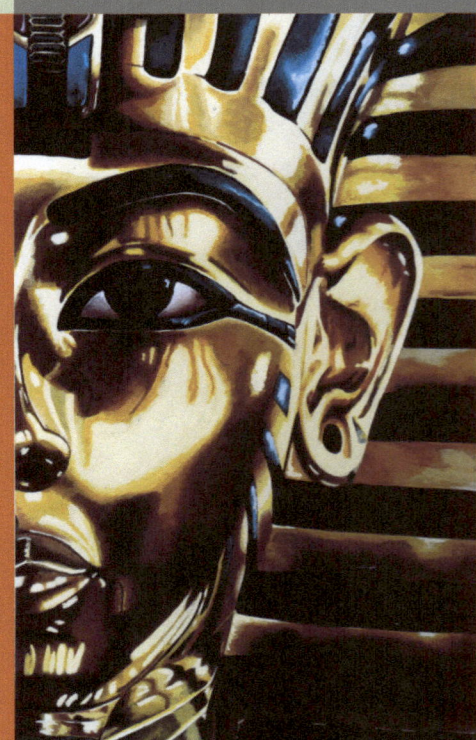

Tutankamón
Acrylic / Cardboard
34 cm x 21 cm
1989

www.ingramcontent.com/pod-product-compliance
Lightning Source LLC
Chambersburg PA
CBHW051829210526
45473CB00005B/1804